MAGIC TRICKS

Fay Presto
MAGIC TRICKS

KINGFISHER

KINGFISHER
Kingfisher Publications Plc,
New Penderel House,
283-288 High Holborn,
London WC1V 7HZ
www.kingfisherpub.com

First published in 1999 by Kingfisher Publications Plc
First published in paperback in 2003

2 4 6 8 10 9 7 5 3 1

1TR/0103/HY/MAR(MAR)/128MA

British Library Cataloguing in Publication Data
A catalogue record is available from the British Library

ISBN 0 7534 0881 3

Printed in China

Senior editor: Sarah Milan
Senior designer: Sarah Goodwin
Production controller: Caroline Jackson
Photographer: Ray Moller
Illustrator: Woody

INTRODUCTION

Hello! My name is Fay Presto. For the last 16 years, I have been having a lot of fun performing magic. One day, after I had been doing some very boring jobs, I decided I would really like to be a magician. So I bought some books about magic, put an act together and off I went. On the way, I discovered some important things: magic is easier than you think it might be; it is not just about tricks, but about people and how you get on with them; and it is about how you present yourself. This book has many new tricks to learn, but it also tells you how to present them, how to present yourself and how to put on a show. It is difficult to have confidence about performing if you haven't done it before. The only way to conquer your fear is to get out there and perform! Magic has been good to me – I have travelled around the world and met many interesting people. And if I have done a particularly good show, I have been rewarded with that most wonderful thing – applause! I hope this book will help you get a start in the world of entertainment, whether you put on a few tricks for some chums or use it as a first step to a glittering career.

CONTENTS

HOW TO USE THIS BOOK

Learn to recognize the features explained below. They have been designed to help you find your way easily around the pages that introduce new tricks and techniques (pages 16–65).

This symbol indicates how easy or difficult the trick is to learn and perform.

easy   **medium**   **difficult**

The introductory text explains what the audience will see. It also tells the magician whether a second person is needed to help with the performance.

The Tips box gives one, or sometimes two, useful hints that the magician should bear in mind when preparing or performing the trick.

The heading SET-UP introduces the steps that the magician must take immediately in advance of the performance. They should be read after the PREPARATION section.

---

60   Anyone at home?

ANYONE AT HOME?

Here is a dramatic trick that works well if there is a lot of space between you and your audience. You will need a small but co-operative assistant – a younger sister or brother will do nicely – and you will need to spend time preparing your main prop – the house from which they will appear.

PREPARATION

YOU WILL NEED:
- a large cardboard box
- a pair of strong scissors
- glue
- coloured card or paints

Tips box

When putting on a show, do this as an opening trick as little people can't sit still for long!

SET-UP

1 Get your assistant to sit quietly under the table before anyone comes into the room. There should be a long tablecloth over the table, so she cannot be seen.

2 Position the roof immediately next to one side of the table and put the main part of the house anywhere that is convenient.

PERFORMANCE

1 Pick up the house and show everyone that it is empty. Then put it down to one side of the roof. There should be no space between the roof, the house and the table.

2 Walk to the front of the stage and keep chatting to your audience about what you are going to do next. Meanwhile, your assistant crawls from under the table, behind the roof and through the secret door into the house. She must be very careful not to move the house as she does this.

The heading PREPARATION is followed by a YOU WILL NEED box, which lists every item needed for the trick. This in turn is followed by several steps showing how to make or prepare your props. The section headed PREPARATION should be read before going on to SET-UP.

This symbol indicates whether the trick is suitable for a close-up, cabaret or stage performance.

close-up

cabaret

stage

Anyone at home?   61

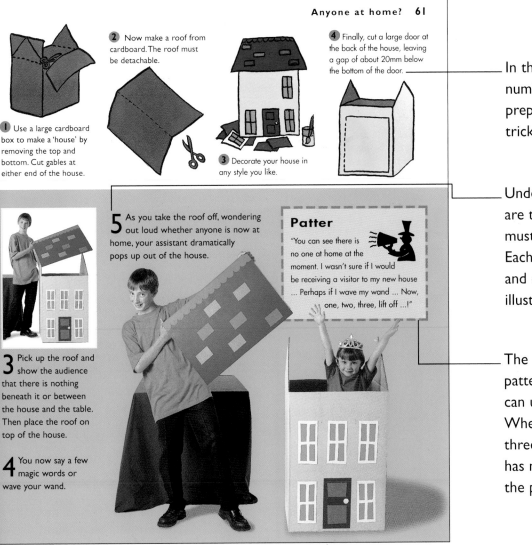

① Use a large cardboard box to make a 'house' by removing the top and bottom. Cut gables at either end of the house.

② Now make a roof from cardboard. The roof must be detachable.

③ Decorate your house in any style you like.

④ Finally, cut a large door at the back of the house, leaving a gap of about 20mm below the bottom of the door.

3 Pick up the roof and show the audience that there is nothing beneath it or between the house and the table. Then place the roof on top of the house.

4 You now say a few magic words or wave your wand.

5 As you take the roof off, wondering out loud whether anyone is now at home, your assistant dramatically pops up out of the house.

Patter

"You can see there is no one at home at the moment. I wasn't sure if I would be receiving a visitor to my new house ... Perhaps if I wave my wand ... Now, one, two, three, lift off ...!"

In the PREPARATION section, numbered steps explain how to prepare the props needed for the trick. Each step is clearly illustrated.

Under the heading PERFORMANCE are the steps that the magician must take to perform the trick. Each step is clearly numbered and explained. The steps are also illustrated with photographs.

The Patter box contains suggested patter, or chat, that the magician can use throughout the trick. Where the text is interrupted by three dots, this means the patter has moved on to the next step of the performance.

USEFUL TIPS

The time will come when you are ready to put on your own show. Before you throw yourself into your act, take some time to read the information on the next few pages. One of the secrets to being a successful magician is to learn the tricks of the trade – discovered the hard way by magicians before you!

THINGS TO REMEMBER

On most pages of this book there are Tips boxes. These contain useful information to help you with a particular trick. On the next six pages there are other general tips and hints that you should try to remember while practising and performing magic.

SMOOTH OPERATOR

When you watch someone perform magic well, it seems as though everything is so easy. In fact, the magician's brain is probably racing, working out which trick to do next, how much more the audience wants and how to get the trick they are doing to work properly! Try to stay calm on the outside even if you can't be calm on the inside.

IT'S SHOWTIME!

Whenever and wherever you perform tricks, you are putting on a *show*. Whether it is on stage at a school concert or at a table after a meal, you will need to give your show some shape by planning a beginning, a middle and an end.

LOCATION

Take a few moments to look at the area where you will be performing. Many rooms have a natural focus. This might be a fireplace, a corner or a door. When you know your exact spot, tailor your programme accordingly. The symbols in this book will help you decide whether a particular trick is suitable for a close-up, cabaret or stage setting (see pages 8–9). Your location should be one of the keys to the tricks you choose.

Make sure that your props, including tables and chairs, are in place before you start.

SEQUENCE

The sequence of tricks you put on in your show is important. You may want to perform one trick in which some silks appear magically from a box, then plan to use these same silks for the next trick. Always finish on a dramatic note and try to leave your audience wanting more!

DON'T TELL

Never repeat a trick, no matter how tempting it may be. The second time around, your audience will be looking to find the secret behind your act. However hard you try, you won't be able to impress them in the same way as you did the first time. Likewise, resist the temptation to tell people the secret of how a trick is done. They will only be disappointed that the magic can be explained away.

DIVERT ATTENTION

If you want to do something without your audience noticing, ask a question. They will automatically look at your face, not at your hands, and you can quickly work some clever magic.

PRACTISE YOUR TECHNIQUE

Remember that practice makes perfect. Use a mirror to see how the tricks will appear to your audience. If you still feel unsure, you can try out a trick on one or two supportive friends.

ENJOY YOURSELF!

Even though you will be thinking about several different things at the same time, remember that the object of putting on a magic show is for you and your audience to have fun. By all means, concentrate on what you are doing, but remember to enjoy yourself too, and the rest will follow naturally.

Use a mirror to show yourself what the audience will see.

ACT THE PART

When you are putting on a show, you'll find that it helps to get yourself and your audience in the right mood if you act the part of a convincing magician. A successful performance is all about presentation – knowing how to act and what to say – so it is worth spending time thinking about the type of magician you want to be.

SPARKLY OR SOLEMN?

Are you a bit of a clown? Well, why not bring out that side of you and dress up as a funny character, cracking jokes to go with your tricks. Or perhaps you're a quiet person? In which case, you could put on a more 'mysterious' act, performing your tricks against a background of appropriate music. After all, it's easier to be who you really are than to try to be someone quite different on stage. On the other hand, you may *prefer* to be someone different to your normal self – it's up to you.

Simple and smart can be highly effective.

DRESSING UP

When you've decided what sort of character you'd like to be, it helps to have a costume. This could be a clown's baggy trousers and red nose, a top hat and cape with stars stuck on or a fairy outfit. Perhaps it could be simply a special jacket or dress that you only put on for performances.

BE PRACTICAL

Don't forget that, whatever you choose to wear, for some tricks you will need a costume with long sleeves in which to hide a prop. Pockets often come in handy for keeping coins and other small objects. But don't let the costume be so fussy or complicated that it gets in your way and distracts you from the real business of performing magic.

WHERE TO PERFORM

Think about where you are going to perform. If you're going to be doing something at the table after a meal, it might look silly if you rush off to put on a sparkly cape and hat. If you are entertaining at a school concert, it is a compliment to your audience to take a bit of trouble with what you are wearing. If you *look* a little special, it is much easier to *be* a little special.

You can hire colourful and flamboyant costumes for that extra special occasion.

PATTER MATTERS

'Patter' is the type of conversation or chatter that magicians and other entertainers often use while they are performing. You'll find it's a good idea to develop some patter of your own, partly to explain to the audience what you're doing (or what you want them to think you're doing!) and partly to distract them from watching you too closely during the tricky parts of your performance. You will find 'Patter' boxes, similar to the one above, with every trick in this book. These can be used as a guide to help you perform.

Patter

"Hello everybody. I'm the friendly wiz that is."

"Good afternoon ladies and gentlemen. I am going to try a few experiments with a pack of cards."

"Is it here, is it there? I'd love to know, it isn't fair."

"Now you see it, now you don't. No point in asking, 'cause tell you I won't."

"I've a little thing to show you. It could be rather fun. It drives me round the corner 'cause I don't known how it's done!"

KEEP PRACTISING

It takes some time to be able to chat easily at the same time as performing a trick – particularly one that requires a lot of dexterity. By practising your patter first with the easier tricks, you'll soon be able to extend this to the more difficult ones.

PROPS AND PUPPETS

The pieces of equipment used by magicians as part of their act are known as 'props' – short for 'theatrical properties'. The simpler ones can be found around the home or 'borrowed' from the audience. Others can be specially prepared in advance or bought from magic shops.

TYPES OF PROP

Most magicians perform with the help of props. These include everyday objects like a pack of cards, pieces of rope or coins. Often, they can be objects that look ordinary but aren't, and these need to be either homemade or bought. Cardboard boxes with false bottoms or secret doors, tubes with hidden compartments and containers that use secret mirrors are all examples of these.

Extra large cards can be found in magic shops.

MAGIC SHOPS

Other props, such as extra large playing cards, magic wands and magician's silks can all be bought from specialist shops. (See page 71 for advice on how to find them). If normal playing cards are too big for your hands, you can buy smaller cards from these shops too.

CAN I BORROW A ...?

Some of the most effective props are those, such as coins or notes, that the magician 'borrows' from members of the audience. Or – if the magician is putting on a show during a meal – those things, such as a serviette, a saltcellar or a glass, that he or she picks up from the table. By using objects that are to hand, it seems to the audience that the magician has not had time to prepare the props and to do anything 'secret' with them – and the apparent spontaneity will add to the realism of the performance. On top of this, the audience won't be suspicious of the props themselves. After all, how can they mistrust something that came from their own back pocket?!

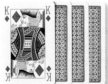

MAKE YOUR OWN PROPS?

Some of the tricks in this book require 'home-made' props. Each of these has clear instructions on how it is made and what equipment you need.

Decorate the props you make with coloured card, shiny tape and stick-on shapes.

For most of them, all you need are inexpensive and easy-to-find objects, such as washing-up liquid bottles, cardboard boxes, margarine tubs and empty matchboxes. Each step is clearly explained and illustrated under the heading PREPARATION.

Now equip yourself with the following:
• a pencil
• a ruler
• scissors
• a set square
• glue
• sticky tape
• coloured card
• paints
and the world of magic is at your fingertips!

MAGIC WITH PUPPETS

Another type of prop that you may want to bring into your act, once you have become confident at learning the tricks, is a hand puppet.

These can only be used with certain types of trick, where you won't be held back by the use of only one hand! But it can be helpful, as well as fun, to have a character on stage with you to talk to, to help you overcome your stage fright or simply to make the trick look more effective.

Tricks you can perform with a puppet:
• Number crunching
• Showing a profit
• I can read you
• That's news to me!
• Rope through you
• Water surprise
• Magical tube
• Flat top, round top
• Twice as rice
• Busted banana
• Glass magic
• Ice-cream queen
• Up your nose!
• Mirror box
• Anyone at home?
• Get lost!

NUMBER CRUNCHING

A member of the audience is asked to write down a series of numbers. When these are added up, they equal a prediction that you have already sealed in an envelope.

PREPARATION

YOU WILL NEED:
- a piece of paper
- a pen
- an envelope

SET-UP

1 On a piece of paper, write down the four-figure number that is two times the current year's date, i.e.
1999 = 3998
2000 = 4000

2 Seal the paper in the envelope. This is your prediction.

Patter

"In here is the answer to a sum we haven't made up yet ... Write the answers to some questions ... Funny, our totals are the same!"

PERFORMANCE

1 Ask a helper to write down the year he was born. (This can be done on a flipchart for a cabaret performance.)

3 Open up the envelope. His total is the same as the number you have already written and sealed there.

2 Below this, he writes the year of an important event in his life, the age he is, or will be, on his birthday this year and the number of years that have passed since the important event. Finally, he writes the total of these four numbers.

SHOWING A PROFIT

Six coins are placed on the page of a large dictionary, opened at the word 'profit'. You tip up the dictionary, sliding the coins onto a helper's hands. But when he counts them, he finds there are ten – he has made a profit of four!

PREPARATION

YOU WILL NEED:
- a large dictionary with stitched binding
- ten small coins

SET-UP

Slide four coins into the spine of an open dictionary. Experiment first to make sure the binding is loose enough for the coins to slide out, but not so loose that they fall out.

Patter

"They always said that if I became a good magician, I could make a profit. Let's turn to the word 'profit' ... Here we are. Now, place these six coins onto the book ... close it ... think about money. Now open it ... How's that for a return!"

PERFORMANCE

1 Open the dictionary at the page with the word 'profit'. Give your helper six coins and ask him to place them on the open page along the crease.

2 Close the book and wave your magic wand over it.

3 Open up the book at the same page and tip it so that the coins fall onto your helper's hands.

4 Ask your helper to count out the coins. He will be amazed to find that there are now ten.

I CAN READ YOU

In this trick, the audience chooses a page number from a book you have apparently chosen at random from the shelves. You go out of the room while a helper reads out the top line of the page. When you come back into the room, you can 'read' their mind by revealing the top line.

PREPARATION

YOU WILL NEED:
- two identical books (dictionaries are best)
- a bookshelf or a pile of other books

SET-UP

1 Set up the room with a shelf of books. Put one of the books you will be using on the shelf.

2 Hide the other identical book outside the room.

Patter

"Pick a page number in this book ... It's important that I don't see or hear what you choose, so I'll go outside ... Concentrate hard ... I'm getting it. It is ..."

PERFORMANCE

1 Pull out a book 'at random' from the shelf and hand it to a helper. Ask him and the audience to agree on a page number.

2 Now leave the room. While you are outside, your helper reads out the top line of the agreed page.

3 Meanwhile, look up the top line of the agreed page in the book you have hidden.

4 On your return, ask the audience to concentrate on the words, then slowly pretend to read their mind by revealing what was written.

THAT'S NEWS TO ME!

In this trick, you cut a strip of newspaper at a point decided on by the audience and a helper. When you open up a sealed envelope, the words written on the paper inside are the same as those on the top line of the newspaper at the point where it was cut.

PREPARATION

YOU WILL NEED:
- a newspaper
- scissors
- a piece of paper
- a pen
- an envelope

SET-UP

1 Cut a strip of continuous text from a newspaper.

2 Write clearly the top line of this text onto a piece of paper and seal it in an envelope.

Patter

"I have a strip of newspaper. Where would you like me to cut it? Say 'stop' at any time ... Would you mind picking up that piece for me ... Read out the top line ... That's what it says in here too!"

PERFORMANCE

1 Hold the strip of newspaper upside down (far enough away from your helper that he can't see it is upside down). Run the scissors up and down and ask your helper to say 'stop' at any point.

2 Cut the strip at the point your helper indicates, and let the bottom part flutter onto the table or the floor.

3 Ask your helper to pick up the piece that has fallen. While he does this, turn the piece in your hand the right way up.

4 Ask your helper to read out the top line of text from the piece he has picked up. Now bring out the envelope — sealed inside are the same words!

ROPE THROUGH YOU

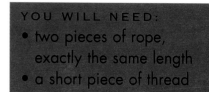

This is a simple and effective trick for a cabaret or stage performance. You will need to call up a volunteer. The audience sees you bring two pieces of rope around the back of your helper and then tie them loosely together at the front. You give both ends a sharp tug and the ropes appear to pass right through the helper's body.

PREPARATION

YOU WILL NEED:
- two pieces of rope, exactly the same length
- a short piece of thread

PERFORMANCE

1 Holding the two ropes in one hand to cover the join, tell the audience you will pass two pieces of rope through your helper.

2 Bring the ropes around the helper's waist, keeping the join out of sight behind his back.

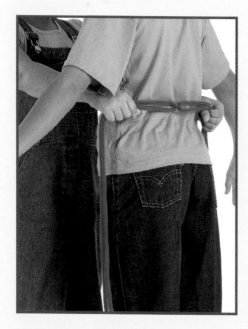

3 Tie the ropes in a loose knot around your helper's waist, but be careful not to pull on the ends too sharply when you do this.

SET-UP

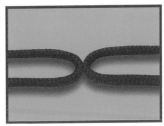

Fold the ropes in half and tie the loops together with a piece of cotton thread. Give the loops a gentle tug to make sure the thread holds.

Patter

"I am always being told that real magicians can saw people in half. I don't need all that expensive equipment – I can do it with two pieces of rope ... Can I have a volunteer? Don't be frightened, it won't hurt ... much! There we are, not too tight, I hope? ... My helper is now surrounded by two rings of the ropes of terror! ... Abracadabra, he's free ... You were inside these loops! Don't bend over too quickly for a week or so!"

5 Hold up the ropes like this to show the loops that went through your helper's waist.

Tips box

1 When setting up your act, lay the ropes on a table with the join out of sight.
2 Use the weakest cotton thread you can find.

4 Now tug the ends of the rope sharply to break the thread. The two pieces of ropes appear to go right through your helper!

ROPE WRIGGLER

In this trick, the audience sees you take three pieces of rope – one short, one of medium length and one long – and transform them into three pieces of rope all of the same length. To get an idea of what the audience will see, practise this effect in front of a mirror.

PREPARATION

YOU WILL NEED:
- a long piece of rope
- scissors
- sticky tape to stop the rope from fraying (optional)

PERFORMANCE

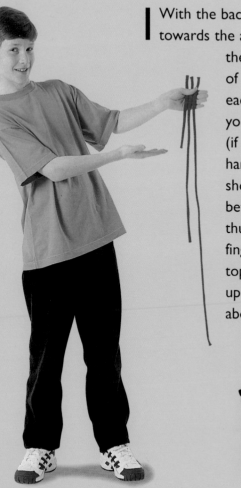

1 With the back of your hand towards the audience, hold the three pieces of rope next to each other in your left hand (if you are right-handed). You should hold them between your thumb and first finger with the top edges sticking up about 4cm above your hand.

2 With the back of your hand still facing the audience, take the bottom end of the short rope and place it next to the top end of the long rope.

3 Twist the bottom end of the short rope over the top of the top edge of the long rope with your thumb. Make sure that no one sees you do this.

4 Now take the bottom end of the medium rope and put it next to the other four ends. Take the bottom end of the long rope and put it next to the other five ends.

Tips box

To add an extra element at the end of this trick, gather the ropes into a bundle and give them to a helper. Ask him or her to hand you back one piece of rope at a time. It will look as though the helper has changed the rope back to pieces of three different lengths.

1 Cut the rope into three pieces: 24cm, 54cm and 86cm long.

2 Put some tape around the ends to stop them from fraying.

Patter

"In my hand I have three pieces of rope, each one a different length. I am going to bring the end of this rope up into my hand ... Now, the ends of the next two ropes ... Can everyone see?

For my next show, I need three pieces of rope all the same length, so why not transform them now? ... I'll take hold of the three ends in one hand and three ends in another, pull them gently apart ... three identical pieces!"

5 Keeping the three ends of rope which are closest to your palm in your left hand, take the other three ends in your right hand.

6 Now pull your hands slowly apart, making sure the loop in your left hand is still hidden.

7 Drop the three ends held in your right hand, and show the audience that all three pieces of rope are the same length.

WATER SURPRISE

This trick is performed in several stages. First of all, you tip plain water through two empty tubes into a mug. You then throw the contents of the mug over the audience, but nothing comes out! You tip the contents of the tubes into a glass and out comes the water – but it has changed colour!

PREPARATION

YOU WILL NEED:
- a plastic cup
- a paperclip
- two pieces of card about 25cm wide and 30cm long
- sticky tape
- scissors
- food colouring
- a glass or other transparent container
- a jug
- a mug or cup (this must not be transparent)

PERFORMANCE

SET-UP

1 Put a drop of food colouring into the plastic cup.

2 Slide the plastic cup inside the top of the smaller tube. Slide the larger tube over the top and hook the cup over both tubes with the paperclip. Make sure the cup is not visible.

1 With your thumb covering the outside of the paperclip, slide out the inside tube with your left hand. The plastic cup should still be hooked to the outside tube.

2 Show the audience that the inside tube is empty. Hold the other tube towards you so that they can't see the cup.

3 Replace the inside tube by sliding it up from underneath. Now slide the outside tube off the bottom, making sure the cup is hooked to the inside tube.

4 This time, show that the outside tube is empty. Remember, hold the other tube so that they can't see the cup.

1 Cut off the rim from the plastic cup. Then straighten the paperclip and fasten it with tape to the side of the cup.

2 Wrap a piece of card, about 25cm wide and 30cm long, around the outside of the cup.

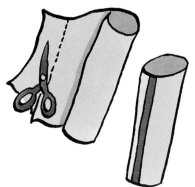

3 Trim the width of the card, leaving an overlapping edge of 5cm, and tape the card down the side to make a tube.

4 From the other piece of card, make a second tube slightly wider than the first (the first tube must be able to slide inside the second tube). Decorate the outside of both tubes.

5 Put the tubes back together again with the cup inside.

6 Holding the tubes above a mug, pour some water from a jug through the tubes into the mug. (The water actually goes into the plastic cup.)

7 Now pretend to throw the mug water at the audience! (Option: have the mug filled with confetti to throw at them.)

8 Wave your wand over the tubes, then turn them upside down and pour the contents of the plastic cup into the empty glass. The water that appears in the glass has changed colour!

Patter

"Two pretty tubes, both of them empty ...
Now, I'll pour water through them into a mug ... See for yourselves! ...
Amazing – the tubes have turned the water green!"

MAGICAL TUBE

You've seen it done before and now you too will be able to perform this classic trick. Your audience will see you pull out several silk scarves from an empty tube. This is a fine cabaret or stage trick that is not difficult to prepare or perform.

PREPARATION

YOU WILL NEED:
- an empty washing-up liquid bottle
- a paper or plastic cup
- black paint
- a paintbrush
- scissors
- glue
- decorative paper or coloured paints
- three or four coloured silks

1 Cut off both ends from the washing-up liquid bottle so that it becomes a tube.

2 Cut off about 5mm from the bottom of the cup. (You may need to cut off more after you have done Step 3.)

3 Position the cup upside down inside the tube just below the tube's rim. You may need to trim the top of the cup if it is too wide.

4 Paint the inside of both the tube and the cup black, then leave them to dry.

5 Put glue on the outside rim of the cup, then position it back inside the tube so that it sticks firmly.

6 Finally, you can decorate the outside of your magical tube with coloured paper or paint.

SET-UP

1 Tie the coloured silks together.

2 Wind the silks round the top end of the tube, tucking them into the gap between the edge of the cup and the tube so that they cannot be seen from the outside.

PERFORMANCE

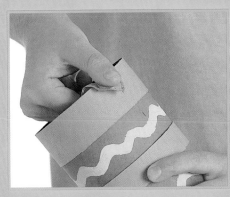

1 Before picking up the tube to show that it is empty, pull out one end of the silk very slightly and hide it beneath your thumb.

2 Show the 'empty' tube to the members of your audience.

Patter

"What you see here is an empty tube. Can everyone see? ... Now I shall weave my magic spell and, lo and behold, we have two – no three – pretty scarves."

3 Wave your wand or sprinkle fairy dust over the tube and say a few magic words.

4 Now pull the silks dramatically out of the tube by transferring the tube to your other hand while still holding onto the silk that was hidden beneath your thumb.

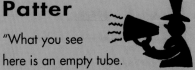

FLAT TOP, ROUND TOP

This is an easy trick that will have your friends and family amazed at your powers of mind-reading. You will be able to pick out the cards that two people have chosen from the pack. All it takes is a little practice in the art of recognizing one type of card from another.

PREPARATION

YOU WILL NEED:
• a pack of cards

To do this trick, you must learn to recognize two different types of card – those with numbers or letters that have a round top and those that have a flat (and also a sharp) top. 3, 5, 7, K are flat, 4 and A are sharp. Look at the examples shown right. With practice, it gets easier to spot which is which.

FLAT (OR SHARP) TOP

3 4 5 7 J K A

ROUND TOP

2 6 8 9 10 Q

SET-UP

1 Sort the pack into two halves, one half consisting of round-topped cards and the other of flat- (and sharp-) topped cards.

2 Now put the two halves back together. (With practice, you'll be able to sort the cards quickly in front of your audience.)

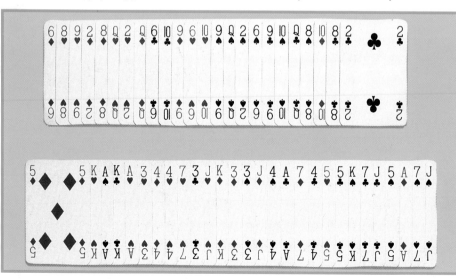

Patter

"I'm going to do a trick so powerful that I don't even touch the cards. Can I have two willing volunteers? Thank you ... Now, each hold out your pack to the other and choose a card. No, wait, I'll stand at the other side of the room so that I can't peek ... Don't forget to memorize your card ... Now, spread them out on the table. Ahh! I am getting the impression of a red card, a high card, a royal card ... the Queen of Diamonds!"

PERFORMANCE

1 Invite up two members of the audience and tell them they will be doing this trick themselves.

2 Tell the audience you are dividing the pack into two. Then, splitting the pack between the two different halves (round-topped and flat-topped), give one half to each of your two helpers.

3 Tell each of the two assistants to select one card from the other person's half pack.

4 They should now look at the card they have chosen, show it to the rest of the audience and memorize it. Make sure that you cannot see the cards they have chosen.

5 Now tell each of them to put the card they have picked into their *own* half pack and to shuffle their cards thoroughly.

6 Ask the helpers to spread out their half packs on the table top. You can now amaze both them and the audience by identifying which cards your two helpers have chosen.

KINGS CHANGE

The audience sees four kings in your hand. You take the King of Clubs and slide it down your arm – it turns into the Ace of Clubs! When you show the cards again, they are all aces.

PREPARATION

YOU WILL NEED:
- four kings, four aces and any other three cards from the pack
- a ruler
- a pencil
- scissors
- glue

1 Glue the back of the King of Clubs to the back of the Ace of Clubs.

2 Cut the other three kings and aces in half diagonally, from the top right to the bottom left corner. Glue the half King of Hearts and the half Ace of Hearts to the *front* of one of the spare cards. Now do the same with the other two kings and aces.

Patter

"Here are four handsome kings ... and here is the King of Clubs on his own. I'd prefer to have a higher card ... Oh look, the Ace of Clubs has turned up! How about these other three? ... They've all followed suit and become aces!"

PERFORMANCE

1 Show the audience that you are holding four kings in your hand.

2 Putting the other cards face down on the table, take the King of Clubs and place it against your arm. Hold it between your thumb and second finger, as shown.

3 Allow the card to flick away from your second finger and run it down your arm, turning it as you do so. The King will appear to change into the Ace of Clubs.

4 Pick up the other three cards and turn them the other way so that the ace halves are uppermost. Put the Ace of Clubs to the front, then show all four aces to the audience.

FEEL THE FORCE

 This technique, known as 'forcing a card', allows you to make someone pick the card you want them to. It will take some practice handling the pack using your stronger hand, but it is a useful and worthwhile technique to learn.

PREPARATION

YOU WILL NEED:
• a pack of cards

SET-UP

Put the card that you want someone to choose onto the top of the pack. Make sure that you have memorized this card.

PERFORMANCE

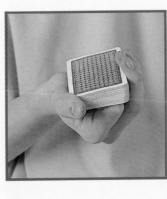

1 Hold the pack face down in your right hand (if you are right-handed) with your thumb on the top corner.

2 Run your thumb down the top corner, flicking through the pack to separate the cards. Ask a helper to tell you when they want you to stop.

3 Using your left hand, open up the pack like a book at the point that you have been told to stop.

4 Lift the top part of the pack between the tips of your left fingers and thumb. As you do this, use the fingers of your right hand to slide the top card off so it falls onto the lower part of the pack.

5 Offer your helper the lower part of the pack so they take the top card. This 'chosen' card is the one you have already memorized.

SENSITIVE SOLE

Once you know how to 'force' your helper to pick a card, there are a number of variants of the trick below that you can perform. In this trick, your helper picks a card 'at random', puts it back into the pack and shuffles the cards. The pack is thrown into the air, you walk over the cards and the chosen card appears by magic in your shoe!

PREPARATION

YOU WILL NEED:
- a pack of cards
- one extra card from another pack

PERFORMANCE

1 Force your helper to choose a card, using the technique described on page 31.

3 Ask him to give the cards a good shuffle before handing the pack back to you.

4 Throw the whole pack up into the air and let them land in a pile on the floor.

2 Your helper should memorize the card then put it back into the pack.

Tips box

If the chosen card lands face up on the floor, you can change the emphasis of the trick as follows: walk over the cards, saying that your feet will tell you when they come in contact with the chosen card. Then bend over, pick up the card and show the audience. For a finale, say that feet are not the only things that come in pairs, and bring out the identical card from inside your shoe.

SET-UP

1 Put an identical card to the one you are going to 'force' your helper to choose into your shoe.

2 Put the actual card your helper is going to choose on the top of the pack.

5 Walk over the cards on the floor, saying that you have sensitive feet.

6 Now stop at the point where you 'feel' the card is and bend down to take off your shoe.

Patter

"Here's a feat of magic I have been walking on, I mean working on, for some time ... Choose a card, remember what it is, and we will return it to the pack ... A good shuffle ... I'll throw the whole pack up into the air ... Now that they're on the ground, my feet should be able to feel your card ... Wow, the card has jumped off the floor and through my shoe ... Upon my soul, was this your card?!"

7 With a flourish, reveal that the chosen card is inside your shoe!

IN-JOG

This is a technique that allows you to keep track of a card that has been freely chosen by a member of the audience. The term 'in-jog' refers to the card – positioned on top of the chosen card – that slightly sticks out towards you in the pack. By keeping the in-jog card under your control as you shuffle, you can always locate the chosen card.

PREPARATION

YOU WILL NEED:
• a pack of cards

PERFORMANCE

1 Ask your helper to select any card she likes.

2 She should look at the card and memorize it.

3 She then puts her chosen card back on top of the pack.

4 Holding the pack in your left hand (if you are right-handed), slide half of the pack out from the bottom with your right hand. You are now ready to do the in-jog.

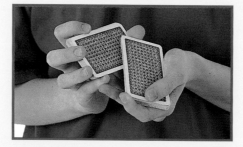

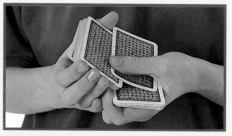

5 With your left thumb, slide off the top card from the half pack that is in your right hand. Make sure this card sticks out towards you by about 1cm.

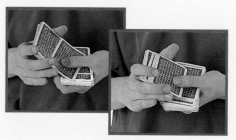

6 Now shuffle the rest of the cards in your right hand onto the half pack in your left hand. Do this quite untidily so the cards are not all neatly lined up.

Tips box

1 You will need to practise this technique until the actions are smooth and undetectable. Watch the angle of your hands, so that the audience doesn't see the break.
2 To find out which is the chosen card, fan the cards out towards you as if you are sorting them and peek at the top card.

7 The pack is now in your left hand with the card chosen by your helper beneath the card that is sticking out towards you (the in-jog card).

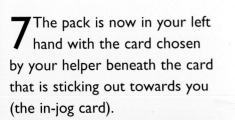

8 Turn the pack sideways in your left hand. With your right thumb, push the top half of the pack away from the bottom half, using the in-jog card.

selected card

9 You will now have a V-shaped break in the pack. The face-down card below the break is the one that your helper has chosen.

10 Shuffle off all the cards above the break into your left hand.

11 Place the bottom half from below the break on top of the other cards in your left hand. The top card is the chosen one.

12 Take the pack back into your right hand and shuffle it by sliding the top card off and putting it to the back of the pack.

13 Now shuffle the whole of the pack until you get to the last card, which you put back on top. You now know the chosen card is back on top.

LIE DETECTOR

You can perform this trick once you have mastered the in-jog technique described on pages 34–35. Your helper picks a card at random from the pack, which you then identify.

PREPARATION

YOU WILL NEED:
• a pack of cards

PERFORMANCE

1 Ask your helper to pick any card from the pack.

2 She should look at the card, memorize it, then put it back on the top of the pack.

3 Shuffle the pack using the in-jog technique (see pages 34–35). At the end, peek at the top card – this is the chosen card.

4 Now give the pack to your helper and ask her to shuffle the pack thoroughly.

5 Tell your helper to turn over the cards one at a time onto the table. She should say 'That is not my card', even when she gets to the card she has picked.

6 Tell your helper that you will know from her voice whether or not she is lying. When she gets to the point where she turns over her chosen card ...

Patter

"I can tell just by the tone of your voice whether you are telling the truth. Pick a card and I will shuffle the pack ... perhaps I was cheating – you shuffle the cards ... Deal them face up, saying each time, 'That is not my card' ... Ah, a little hesitation – that was your card."

7 ... tell her you know she is lying and point to the right card.

KEY CARD

This is another technique for finding out which card your helper has freely selected. It is similar in function to the in-jog technique (see pages 34–35), but is much easier to learn and perform.

PREPARATION

YOU WILL NEED:
- a pack of cards

SET-UP

Memorize the card at the bottom of the pack. This is the 'key card'.

Patter

"Pick a card. We must lose it in the pack. Say 'stop' anywhere you like ... Here? Put your card back in the pack ... I can see a black card, a card with the number five – the Five of Clubs!"

PERFORMANCE

1 Ask your helper to pick any card from the pack. He should look at the card and remember it.

2 Deal a few cards onto the table and ask your helper to say 'stop' at any time.

3 Now tell him to put his selected card onto the top of the pile on the table.

4 Put the rest of the cards on top. The key card is now on top of the chosen card.

5 Look at the cards as if you are concentrating and slowly 'guess' the chosen card. Alternatively, you can glance through the cards, see which one has been chosen, and perform a similar 'guessing' trick, e.g. Lie detector (see page 36).

TWICE AS RICE

In this impressive trick, the audience sees you fill an empty margarine tub to the brim with uncooked rice. You then place an identical margarine tub upside down over the top. When you take the top tub away, the rice has doubled in quantity.

PREPARATION

YOU WILL NEED:
- two identical empty margarine tubs and tops with sides that taper slightly
- scissors
- glue
- sticky tape
- a jug of uncooked rice
- a deep-sided tray
- coloured card or paints

1 Carefully cut round the lip of one of the margarine tub lids, leaving a flange (edge) so that it can be glued easily.

2 Glue the lid into one of the tubs about halfway down.

3 Optional: decorate both tubs, but make sure they are identical.

Patter

"I am going to fill this tub with rice. Oops, too much, I just need to level it off with my wand ... Now it is full to the brim ... You see here another tub – empty this time ... I'll place this second empty tub on the top ... Now I can show the rice and tubs to the frozen north ... to the mysterious east ... to the sunny south ... and to the wild, wild west ... And now, having been all round the world ... our rice may not be twice as nice, but it is twice as rice!"

PERFORMANCE

1 Fill the unaltered tub above the brim with rice.

2 Level off the rice with your wand, allowing any spillage to fall onto the tray.

3 Remove the lid from the second tub, keeping the open top away from your audience.

4 Place the altered tub upside down on top of the tub that is filled with rice.

5 Turn the tubs sideways, holding them firmly together, and show them to all four corners of the room.

6 When you turn to face your audience, turn the tubs upright onto the tray, making sure the altered tub is now at the bottom.

7 As you dramatically remove the top tub, the rice will spill out all over the tray. You have apparently doubled its volume.

CEREAL KILLER

You open up a packet of cereal in front of the audience, but there is only one tiny flake of cereal left inside. You demonstrate that the packet is empty by opening the bottom and allowing the audience to look right through it. Then you close the bottom and the top and tap your wand on the packet. When you open up the top of the packet again, you can pour out a full portion of cereal into the bowl.

PREPARATION

YOU WILL NEED:
- two identical cereal packets
- enough cereal to fill a bowl
- glue
- scissors
- velcro
- a bowl
- a spoon

1 Open the flaps of both packets. Cut a section from one packet, from the bottom corner to a width of 4cm at the top.

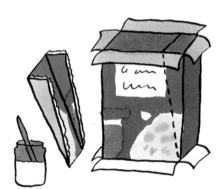

2 Turn the section inside out and spread glue on its outside edges. Stick it firmly inside the unaltered cereal packet.

3 Cut two strips of velcro and glue them to the bottom flaps of the packet. Now close up the packet at the bottom and fasten.

SET-UP

Pack the secret compartment tightly with cereal. Cover the cereal with one of the side flaps and try shaking the box — it must not rattle. If it does, pack it even more tightly with cereal. Then close up the packet.

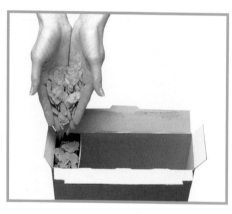

Tips box

When you open the box to pour out the single flake of cereal at the start of the trick, hold your fingers firmly over the side flap to hide the secret compartment and to keep it closed.

PERFORMANCE

Patter

"After a hard day's magicking, I really need a bowl of cereal. Oh no, someone has been here before me ... Look, there is nothing left in the packet ... Perhaps if I really imagine a lovely full bowl of cereal ... Yes, out it comes! Now, where's the milk?"

1 Open the cereal packet and pour out the single flake of cereal into the bowl. Look sad when you see that this is all that is left.

3 Close up the flaps of the cereal packet and tap the packet with your magic wand.

4 Now open the top of the packet, tip it up and pour out a whole bowlful of cereal!

2 Open up the bottom flaps of the cereal packet and, pointing the base towards the audience, show them that the packet is completely empty.

THROUGH THE TABLE

Here's a vanishing trick that can be performed right under the eyes of your audience. It will take a bit of practice in front of a mirror to get the timing right, but you'll find that, once perfected, it is a very effective trick that will impress your friends enormously.

PREPARATION

YOU WILL NEED:
- a saltcellar
- a paper serviette
- a small coin

PERFORMANCE

1 Place a coin on the table and tell the audience you are going to push it right through the table.

3 Position your hands on the serviette either side of the saltcellar so that you have the saltcellar in your grip.

4 Tell the audience that after a count of three, the coin will go through the table. Now move the saltcellar, covered by the serviette, back and forth from its position on the table to a position just above your lap to see if the coin has gone.

2 Place the saltcellar on top of the coin, then cover the saltcellar with the serviette 'for safety reasons'.

5 Move the saltcellar back and forth three times, checking to see if the coin is still there. Click the saltcellar onto the coin each time.

If you can't find a saltcellar with a pointed top, you can use another object that is similar in size and that tapers at the top.

Tips box

As an extra element to this trick, you can reach under the table at the end of the trick – as if you are reaching for something on the floor – and bring up the saltcellar hidden on your lap. Show the audience that it has gone right through the table.

6 On the fourth count, at the point where the saltcellar and serviette are above your lap, gently let the saltcellar drop into your lap and return the serviette, still holding its shape, to its original position above the coin.

7 Release the serviette and, before your audience realizes the saltcellar is no longer there ...

8 ... bang your hand flat onto the serviette – the coin is still there, but the saltcellar has gone!

Patter

"I am going to push this coin right through the table with this saltcellar ... We'll cover it with a serviette as it looks a bit fragile ... On the count of three, the coin should disappear. One ... two ... three ... Whoops, the coin is still there, but the saltcellar has disappeared."

BUSTED BANANA

By using a technique called 'magician's choice' – which allows you to make your helper choose the number you want him to – you can work this piece of clever magic. The audience sees a banana, once peeled, fall into the same number of pieces as the number chosen by your helper.

PREPARATION

YOU WILL NEED:
- stiff paper or card
- a thick pen
- scissors
- a bunch of bananas
- a darning needle

1 Cut out four pieces of card. They should be about the same size as a playing card.

2 Write a number on each card. You can choose any numbers, but one of them must be a 3.

Patter

"Choose two numbers. Two and four? I'll remove these cards ... Now another number. Three? Okay, I'll take away the card you didn't want ... Now, banana, which number is left ... Sorry, can't hear you. Peel you, why? Oh, alright ... Ah, the answer is on the inside."

Tips box

1 The banana can fall into three, four or five pieces. Vary the number at different shows in case the same person turns up more than once.

2 For a cabaret or stage show, use larger cards and an easel to display the numbers.

SET-UP

Just before the performance (not too early or the banana will go brown), stick the darning needle into one of the bananas a third of the way from the top. Wriggle the needle gently from side to side. In the same way, make a second hole with the needle a third of the way from the bottom of the banana.

PERFORMANCE

1 Place the four cards face up on the table in no particular order. Then ask your helper to choose any two numbers.

2 If your helper has not picked the 3, take away the two cards he has picked. If he has picked the 3 as one of his two cards, take the other two cards off the table. (You need to be left with the 3 on the table.)

3 Ask your helper to pick one of the two remaining cards. (Again, you need to be left with the 3 on the table.)

4 If he has pointed to the 3, take away the other card. If he has not pointed to the 3, take away the card he has pointed to.

5 Hand your helper a banana (the one you prepared earlier), and tell him the banana will know which number he has chosen.

6 Your helper should take the banana and peel it. It will fall into three pieces.

GLASS MAGIC

You need a member of the audience to participate in this trick. After showing your helper a coin at the bottom of a wine glass, you ask him to cover the top of the glass while you tap his hand from underneath with a second coin. This coin appears alongside the first coin in the glass.

PREPARATION

YOU WILL NEED:
- a bowl-shaped wine glass
- three coins, one large and two small (the small coins must look the same)

PERFORMANCE

1 Slide a small coin, hidden beneath a larger coin, down the side of the glass.

3 Tip up the glass onto the palm of your helper's hand. Again, he will see only the larger coin.

2 Now swirl the glass to show that there is only one coin in it. The smaller coin should stay hidden under the larger one. Show your helper the 'single' coin.

4 Your helper should now hold the glass upside down between his palms. Take the other small coin and tell your audience that it will work its way up into the glass through your helper's hand.

SET-UP

Make sure you have the right combination of glass and coins before you begin. Experiment by swirling two coins – the larger one above a smaller one – around the glass.

5 With the second small coin visible between your thumb and first finger, knock your helper's hand from underneath. The jolt will make the smaller coin hidden in the glass appear on top of the larger coin. Quickly hide the small coin that you were holding in your hand by dropping it into your closed palm and, from there, onto your lap or in your pocket.

ICE-CREAM QUEEN

This trick starts off with a member of the audience selecting one card from a pack. You then place the pack inside a cone made of folded paper. When the cone is opened up, the pack of cards has vanished, but when you turn the opened cone around, a large picture of the card chosen by your helper is stuck to the side.

PREPARATION

YOU WILL NEED:
- two squares of coloured craft paper (30cm x 30cm)
- decorative sticky tape
- glue
- a pack of cards
- a giant Queen of Hearts (or any other large card)

1 Tape together the two squares of craft paper, leaving a 12cm opening in one corner.

2 Glue the large Queen of Hearts (or other chosen card) to the centre of one side of the squares.

3 Make three folds in the squares, as shown. When folded up, this should make a cone.

Patter

"This is an audience participation trick. First of all, my friend will choose a card and show you what it is ... Now she shuffles the pack – thank you – and I place the pack into this cone ... Now, if you all shout 'jump', the card my friend has chosen will jump out of the cone ... Oops, that was a bit too loud. The whole pack of cards has jumped out of the cone. No, there is nothing there ... all except one card, that is. Was your card ... the Queen of Hearts?"

PERFORMANCE

1 Use the forcing technique described on page 31 to make your helper pick the Queen of Hearts. She should show the card to the audience, then replace it anywhere in the pack.

described on page 31

forcing technique described on page 31

Tips box ... page 31

Tips box

1 In order to make the secret pocket harder to spot, stick the decorative tape onto the inside edges of the opening.
2 When you fold the paper into a cone, keep the secret opening facing towards you.

3 Look into the cone and explain that when the audience shouted 'jump', they frightened away all the cards. Open the cone to show that the pack has vanished. (Keep the large card facing towards you.)

2 Ask your helper to shuffle the pack, then you drop it into the hidden pocket of the cone. It should look as if you are placing the pack into the middle of the cone.

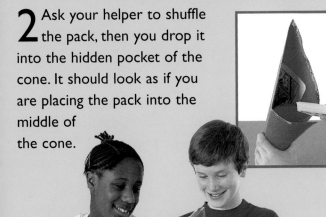

4 With a smile, say there is one card left and, turning the cone around, ask your helper if this was the card she picked.

LINKING SILKS

The vanishing cone (pages 48–49) is useful for making small objects appear and disappear. Using three cones, you can perform the following trick. You place three cones into three glasses. Then you place one silk scarf into each cone. On opening up the first cone, the silk has vanished. The same thing happens when you open up the second cone. But when you open up the third cone, you pull out all three silks linked together.

PREPARATION

YOU WILL NEED:
- six squares of coloured craft paper, 30cm x 30cm (i.e. two green, two yellow, two blue)
- three tall, thin glasses in which to rest the cones
- six silks (two each of three different colours)

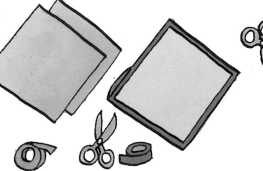

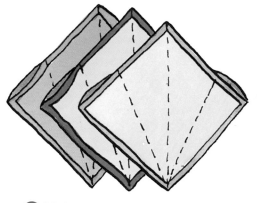

1 Tape together two pairs of craft paper squares, leaving a gap of 12cm in one corner (see page 48).

2 Tape together the third pair of squares (the yellow pair is shown here), leaving two 12cm gaps.

3 Make three folds in each of the squares as shown, then fold them into three cones.

SET-UP

1 Tie three different coloured silks together and put the remaining three separate silks onto one side ready for use.

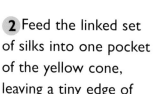

2 Feed the linked set of silks into one pocket of the yellow cone, leaving a tiny edge of the top silk sticking out.

3 Lay the three paper squares flat on the table.

PERFORMANCE

1 Take each square, fold it into a cone and place one cone in each glass.

4 Open up the blue cone and show that the first silk has vanished. Open up the green cone and show that the next silk has vanished.

2 Place one silk into the secret pocket of the blue cone. It should look to the audience as if you are placing the silk into the middle of the cone. Then place another silk into the green cone pocket.

5 Hold the yellow cone firmly in the glass with one hand and, with the other hand, pull out the chain of linked silks.

3 Now place the third silk into the empty pocket of the yellow cone. At the same time, make sure that the top edge of the linked set of silks (in the other pocket) is hanging over the edge of the cone.

DEVIL'S HANDCUFFS

The two ends of a piece of rope are tied snugly around both of your wrists by one or two helpers. You then take a bangle in one hand, and hide both hands and the bangle under a large silk scarf. Seconds later, your helpers remove the scarf – and the bangle is dangling from the rope!

PREPARATION

YOU WILL NEED:
- a piece of rope about 1m long
- a large silk scarf
- two identical bangles
- a long-sleeved top

SET-UP

Slide one bangle up your arm, hiding it beneath your sleeve.

PERFORMANCE

1 Ask two helpers to tie one end of a piece of rope around one wrist and the other end around the other wrist.

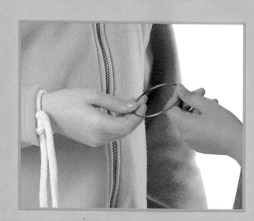

2 Ask one helper to pass you the bangle, and tell the audience you will make this appear on the rope with your hands still tied.

Patter

"Could I have two volunteers who know how to tie a strong knot. Thank you ... Tie each end of this rope around my wrists – see, I've been handcuffed ... Now pass me that bangle ... and cover my hands with this scarf ... Now, here's a knotty problem. How can I get the bangle onto the rope without untying the knots? ... On the count of three, take the scarf away ... One ... two ... three ... Magic!"

5 Now ask your helpers to take the scarf away. Hold up your arms with a flourish and show the bangle dangling from the rope.

Tips box

1 For a close-up performance, slide the bangle off your arm while it is under the table.
2 To prove the knots haven't been untied, ask a helper to mark the rope.

3 Tell your helpers to cover your hands with the scarf. They should hold up the ends of the scarf.

4 With your hands out of sight, lose the bangle in your pocket or under your clothes. Then slide the hidden bangle down your sleeve on top of the rope.

MIRROR BOX

The box described here is a handy prop which can be used for several appearing and vanishing tricks (see page 56 and pages 66–69). It has two compartments, but because of the mirror angled inside it, the audience only ever sees one. The other 'invisible' compartment can be used to hide silks or other objects.

PREPARATION

YOU WILL NEED:
- a mirror (this can be small, i.e. approx. 8cm x 5cm) or larger (i.e. approx. 20cm x 15cm)
- some strong card
- a ruler
- a set square
- scissors
- a craft knife
- a pencil
- glue
- coloured paper or paints
- two fasteners

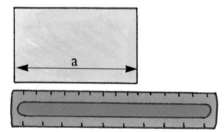

1 Measure the longest side of the mirror. This is measurement (a).

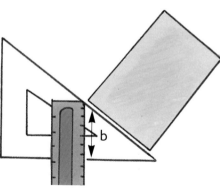

2 Hold the short side of the mirror against the long side of the set square. Use a ruler to measure the drop. This is measurement (b).

3 On the card, draw two vertical lines. The distance between the lines should be the same as measurement (a). Draw a line across the top joining the vertical lines. Leave a gap of 1cm, then draw four more horizontal lines, each the width of (b) apart.

Tips box

1 Buy the mirror first before making the box. It can be the size of a compact mirror (small enough to put in a handbag). But if you are putting on a stage show, you will need a bigger box, so buy a piece that measures about 20cm x 15cm.

2 When you are telling the audience what you are doing, remember not to refer to the box as a mirror box!

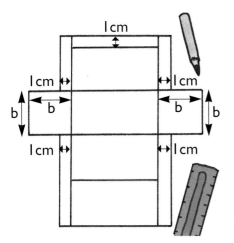

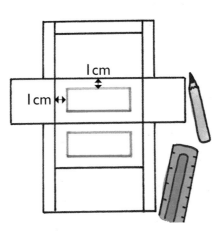

4 Draw a square on each end of the second rectangle from the top, as shown. Then draw a line 1cm wide around the edges of the three remaining rectangles.

5 Draw a smaller rectangle inside each of the two central rectangles. The gap around the edge of the smaller rectangles should be 1cm. Cut round three sides of these rectangles, as shown here in blue.

6 Draw lines across the corners of the three large rectangles to mark the edges of the tabs. Now cut out your box following the blue dotted and black lines shown here. Score along the red lines using a ruler and a pair of closed scissors.

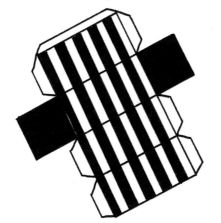

7 Fold up the sides and one end of the box and glue in the tabs. Then slide the mirror diagonally into the box and fold up the other end, sticking the tabs in place.

8 To help create the illusion of an empty box, it is a good idea to line the inside with stripey paper. This is easiest to do after Step 4, before you use the scissors.

9 Now decorate your box. If you are using coloured paper to stick onto the outside, it is also best to do this after Step 4. Stick fasteners onto the two doors.

MIRROR MAGIC

The audience sees you place four silks one by one into an empty box. When you pull them out, they are linked together.

PREPARATION

YOU WILL NEED:
- the Mirror box (pp54–55)
- eight silks (two each of four different colours)

SET-UP

1 Tie four different-coloured silks together and place them into the box through the door at the top.

2 Put the other four silks onto the table ready for use.

Patter

"You can see that this box has nothing in it ... one by one, I will place each of these silk scarves into the box ... now for a bit of magic ... when I open the door, the scarves have joined forces!"

PERFORMANCE

1 Open the door at the front of the box and show the audience that there is nothing inside.

2 Place the first silk into the box through the front door.

3 Now place the next three silks into the box one by one.

4 Close up the box and wave your magic wand over it.

5 Open the top door of the box and, with a flourish, pull out the silks tied together.

UP YOUR NOSE!

This trick works well in a stage or cabaret setting. If you are feeling confident, you can perform it close-up. The audience sees you make a wand disappear halfway up your nose – or even into your ear! Follow the instructions below carefully.

PREPARATION

YOU WILL NEED:
- black card (15cm x 5cm)
- white card (6cm x 4cm)
- glue
- scissors

1 Roll up a piece of black card to make a narrow tube about 15cm in length. Then stick down the edge.

2 Cut out a piece of white card 1cm x 5cm. Wrap it around one end of the tube and stick it in place.

3 Wrap more white card (1.5cm x 5.5cm) around the other end. This must be loose enough to slide up and down. Stick down the edge.

PERFORMANCE

2 As you move the sliding white end up towards your nose, keep the protruding black end (shown here) hidden behind your hand.

1 Place the fixed end of the wand against your nose with the white hidden beneath your fingers. Keeping the other white end in view, slide it slowly up the tube.

Patter

"Do you know why they call a magic wand 'magic'? Because it has a great disappearing trick of its own ... Now you see it ... now you only see a bit of it ... "

3 Slide the white end back to its starting position, take the wand away and show that your nose and the wand are fine!

SHAKE THAT BOX

The audience sees you take out a paperclip from one of three matchboxes. Then you mix up the boxes and ask a helper to point to the one with the paperclip in it. You rattle the box, but there is no sound. Now you point to another matchbox. This rattles and, when you open it up, there is the paperclip! Each time you mix up the boxes, your helper picks the wrong box.

PREPARATION

YOU WILL NEED:
- four empty matchboxes
- four paperclips
- an elastic band
- invisible double-sided sticky tape

SET-UP

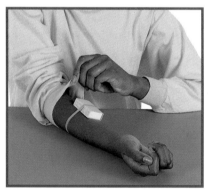

Put a paperclip into the fourth matchbox and fasten this to your right arm with the elastic band. Then roll down your sleeve to hide the box.

Tips box

You can do this trick as many times as you like – just remember to use the correct hand to shake the boxes!

PERFORMANCE

1 Open any box, take out the paperclip and show it to the audience and to your helper. Then put back the paperclip and close up the box.

2 Shake the box you have closed with your right hand. The audience will hear the paperclip up your sleeve rattling and believe it is the one in the box.

3 Tell your helper to watch carefully while you mix around the matchboxes several times.

1 Stick some invisible double-sided sticky tape to the bottom of three of the matchboxes.

2 Press a paperclip onto the sticky tape. Make sure the boxes don't rattle when you shake them.

Patter

"Use your memory to beat the magician. Three boxes, one paperclip ... I'll mix up the boxes ... Which one has the paperclip in it? This one? Sure? ... Sorry, no paperclip in here ... I say it's in this one ... Here it is ... Now, let's try this again!"

6 Tell your helper that the paperclip is in another matchbox. Demonstrate this by shaking a matchbox of your choice, but make sure you use your right hand so that the paperclip rattles.

4 Ask your helper to point to the matchbox that she believes contains the paperclip.

5 Shake the matchbox that your helper pointed to using your left hand. There is no sound and you tell her the box is empty.

7 Now open up the matchbox you have just shaken and take out the paperclip from the bottom.

ANYONE AT HOME?

Here is a dramatic trick that works well if there is a lot of space between you and your audience. You will need a small but co-operative assistant – a younger sister or brother will do nicely – and you will need to spend time preparing your main prop – the house from which they will appear.

PREPARATION

YOU WILL NEED:
- a large cardboard box
- a pair of strong scissors
- glue
- coloured card or paints

Tips box

When putting on a show, do this as an opening trick as little people can't sit still for long!

SET-UP

1 Get your assistant to sit quietly under the table before anyone comes into the room. There should be a long tablecloth over the table, so she cannot be seen.

2 Position the roof immediately next to one side of the table and put the main part of the house anywhere that is convenient.

PERFORMANCE

1 Pick up the house and show everyone that it is empty. Then put it down to one side of the roof. There should be no space between the roof, the house and the table.

2 Walk to the front of the stage and keep chatting to your audience about what you are going to do next. Meanwhile, your assistant crawls from under the table, behind the roof and through the secret door into the house. She must be very careful not to move the house as she does this.

1 Use a large cardboard box to make a 'house' by removing the top and bottom. Cut gables at either end of the house.

2 Now make a roof from cardboard. The roof must be detachable.

3 Decorate your house in any style you like.

4 Finally, cut a large door at the back of the house, leaving a gap of about 20mm below the bottom of the door.

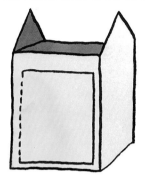

3 Pick up the roof and show the audience that there is nothing beneath it or between the house and the table. Then place the roof on top of the house.

4 You now say a few magic words or wave your wand.

5 As you take the roof off, wondering out loud whether anyone is now at home, your assistant dramatically pops up out of the house.

Patter

"You can see there is no one at home at the moment. I wasn't sure if I would be receiving a visitor to my new house ... Perhaps if I wave my wand ... Now, one, two, three, lift off ...!"

BIG BOX

In order to perform the trick explained on pages 64–65, you need to make the Big box shown here. Before you start, think of who you can use to help you perform the trick. This will help you decide how large the box needs to be.

trick explained on pages 64–65

PREPARATION

YOU WILL NEED:
- a cardboard box measuring approx. 80cm x 50cm
- two pieces of cardboard, approx. 80cm x 50cm
- a craft knife or strong scissors
- glue or sticky tape
- coloured paper or paints
- rope or strong sticky tape for the handle

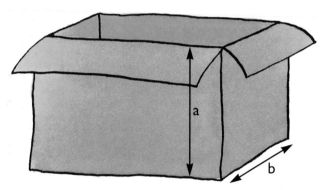

1 Find a large cardboard box that has square ends. In other words, its height (a) must measure the same as its depth (b). It should be wider than it is tall.

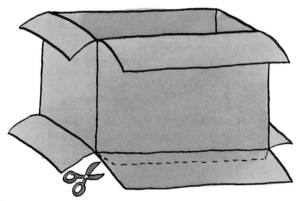

2 Open up the bottom flaps and cut off the two shorter flaps and one of the longer ones. Trim the remaining flap to approximately 4cm.

Tips box

1 This will be easier to make if you have two identical boxes. You can then cut the two pieces described in Step 4 from the second box.
2 When practising this trick, check that your assistant will not be visible from anywhere in the audience.

3 Now paint the inside of the box black, including its flaps. Remember that the side with the 4cm flap will form the front of the box for your trick.

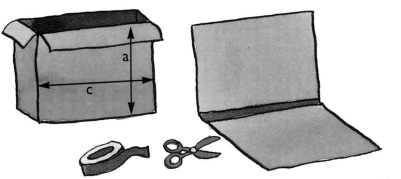

4 Now take the two pieces of cardboard and trim them to 1cm less than the width of the box (c) and 1cm less than the height of the box (a). Stick the two pieces together at right angles to each other.

5 Make a handle from rope or from the sticky tape and fasten it to the inside of the upper piece of card in the position shown. Paint the joined pieces of card black on both sides.

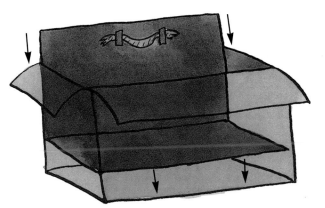

6 Slide the two pieces of card into the box as shown. The side with the handle on should be facing away from the front panel of the box. Where the two pieces of card are joined, they should rest on the 4cm flap.

7 Now decorate the outside of your box. You can keep it plain if you prefer, but this risks drawing attention to the painted flaps.

8 Finally, you should practise with your assistant the following technique: he sits on the false bottom of the box, holding onto the handle; you tip the box forwards and the false side (with the handle on it) now becomes the bottom of the box, with your assistant holding it in position.

GET LOST!

This trick is an illusion that works well as an opening trick in a stage setting using the Big box shown on pages 62–63. You will need an assistant – with whom you have practised the trick in advance – small enough to hide behind the box but old enough to work the box's magic door. The audience sees you open up the box and tip it forwards to show it is empty. Then you close the box. When you open it up again, your assistant magically appears.

PREPARATION

YOU WILL NEED:
- the Big box (pp62–63)
- a solid table on which to perform the trick

PERFORMANCE

1 Open the box, tilt it forwards and show the audience that it is empty. (Your assistant sits behind it, holding the false bottom in place.)

2 Carefully tilt the box back onto the table. Your assistant pushes the false bottom forwards and ducks into the box.

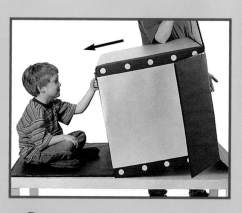

3 Now close the top flaps of the box.

SET-UP

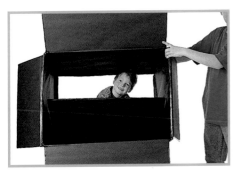

1 Practise tilting the box forwards and backwards with your assistant holding onto the handle. He should be behind the box when it is tilted forwards and inside it when it is standing on the table.

2 Before the audience comes in, get your assistant to sit inside the box, facing the front and holding onto the handle (see page 63).

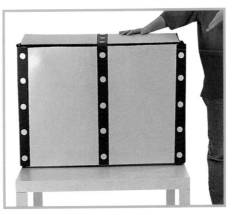

(see page 63).

Patter

"What you see here is an empty box. Can everyone see? Empty on the inside, empty on the outside ... Now I'll close it up ... and say a few magic words. Don't you think it would be fun to conjure up someone who can help me with the rest of my act ... here we go again, I'll open up the box to see who or what appears ... here comes trouble!"

Tips box

You can perform this trick at the start of your act, then work with your assistant during the show. To finish the act, you can reverse the trick by making your assistant climb back into the box and disappear!

5 Open the box without tilting it forwards. Your assistant makes a dramatic appearance!

4 Say a few magic words over the closed box.

PUTTING ON A SHOW

There are several important things to consider when preparing for your show. From planning your routine to packing up your props, from setting up the stage to preparing your finale, there are a number of separate elements that will each require careful consideration well in advance of the actual performance.

Ideas for a stage show
1 Mirror box with rope
2 Rope through you (helper)
3 Ice-cream queen (helper)
4 Magical tube (puppet)
5 Mirror box with ribbon fountain

PLAN YOUR PROGRAMME

Choose the tricks that you are going to perform well in advance of your show. The setting of your performance should be one of the first things you consider when deciding on your programme.

Think about lighting, music and how to display your props. A prompt card is useful to remind you of your routine.

There are three suggested programmes in this section. The one above is suitable for a stage setting, and the five tricks listed are photographed over the next four pages. Two further programmes are shown on page 68 — one for a cabaret setting and one for a close-up setting.

PREPARING PROPS

Before you pack up your props, check that you have carried out all of the PREPARATION steps and as many of the SET-UP steps as you can do in advance. For example, if you are planning to make a ribbon fountain and a rope appear from the same Mirror box, you must make sure you have packed the box with both objects in the right order. When packing, be careful how you arrange the props. Some are more fragile than others and may need extra packaging.

CHOOSE YOUR SPOT

Wherever your performance is going to be, it is important that you familiarize yourself with the actual spot that will form your 'stage' well in advance. If it is in a room rather than on stage, look for the room's natural focus. Think about where your audience can sit so that they are comfortable and have a good view.

SETTING UP

It is often a good idea to set up your 'stage' with some extra lighting. Make sure that the light doesn't come from directly behind you, as this will put you into shadow. If you are using music, think about what you are playing and what you will use to play it on. For both lighting and music, you will need access to a power socket. You may also need certain furniture props, such as a generous-sized table, perhaps with a long cloth over the top.

The magician uses the rope that he caused to appear in his opening trick as the main prop for the trick that follows.

MAKE AN IMPACT

Now that your audience is sitting comfortably, the lights are on and the music is playing, it is time for the first trick of your act. Choose something that is visually dramatic – here the magician makes ropes appear from the Mirror box.

NEXT ...

Where possible, think of ways to make one trick flow smoothly into another. This can be done by using the prop that magically appeared in the previous trick. Here the magician uses the rope he conjured out of the Mirror box for his next trick, Rope through you.

YOUR HELPER

For some of the tricks you choose, you will need an assistant, or helper. Often, this needs to be someone that you choose at random from the audience. When choosing the person to help you with your act, pick out someone who looks as if they are genuinely willing to come forward.

Look for a willing volunteer to help you.

Not everyone wants to be in the limelight nor run the risk of being caught unawares. For certain tricks, your assistant will need to be someone who shares your knowledge of the trick and with whom you have practised in advance of the show. If your assistant is very young or is hiding in a tight corner somewhere, use them as early on as you can. Always be courteous to your helper – it is a mistake to make them look stupid for falling for the trick. Before they go back to their seat, thank them for participating in the show.

Below are two suggested programmes. One is for a cabaret and the other for a close-up show.

USING PUPPETS

To introduce some variety, you may decide to use a puppet to help you with your show. Pick a trick where you won't be hindered if you use a puppet on one of your hands, and practise the type of patter you and the puppet will use.

YOUR FINALE

For your final trick, try and finish on a dramatic note, so that you leave your audience wanting more. The trick shown here involves bringing a ribbon fountain from out of the Mirror box. (You make a ribbon fountain by laying a long length of ribbon into the box in a series of gentle zigzag folds). Be prepared to have one more trick ready just in case the audience asks for an encore. Whatever happens, don't be tempted to explain or repeat any of your tricks!

Puppets can be used to help your act along.

Producing a ribbon fountain from the box is a dramatic finale (right).

Ideas for a cabaret show

1 Anyone at home? (helper)
2 Devil's handcuffs (helper)
3 Water surprise (helper)
4 Twice as rice
5 Linking silks

Ideas for a close-up show

1 Busted banana (helper)
2 Glass magic (helper)
3 Number crunching (helper)
4 Lie detector (helper)
5 Through the table

GLOSSARY

Magicians use a number of specialist words to describe their gimmicks and techniques. Below are listed most of the new words you will come across, with an explanation of what they mean.

control A method of keeping tabs on a card that has been selected.

ditch To drop or lose something quietly and without being seen.

fake (or feke) Something that looks normal but that has been adjusted to help you do a trick.

fanning powder (zinc stearate) A fine powder rubbed onto playing cards so they are easier to handle.

finale The end of a trick or act.

force A method of making someone pick the card that you want them to.

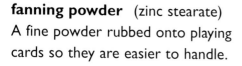

gimmick A secret piece of equipment.

illusion A large trick that involves sawing people up or making them appear or disappear.

index (indices) The numbers and symbols in the corner of a playing card.

lapping Dropping something secretly onto your lap.

levitation The illusion of someone or something floating without visible means of support.

load An object or objects produced from somewhere secret.

misdirection Any method used to make the audience look away while you are carrying out a move you don't want them to see.

move The actual execution of a secret movement.

palming The concealment of an object in the palm of the hand.

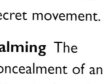

patter The chat or description of a trick while performing.

production A trick where things are made to appear from thin air or empty boxes.

props Any equipment used to perform a trick.

pull A gimmick used to vanish an object by pulling it up a sleeve or under a jacket.

routine The order of events in a trick or the order of tricks in a show.

set-up A secret arrangement of equipment before the performance.

silk A silk scarf or piece of fine fabric of varying size.

sleight of hand An undetected movement of fingers to accomplish the move of a trick.

square up To tidy up cards into a neat pack.

steal To secretly remove something from where it is hidden.

switch To secretly exchange one thing for another.

talk An accidental clicking made by something hidden, which gives away its presence to the audience, e.g. the clicking of coins in a hand.

WHERE TO GO NEXT

You may think it will be difficult to find out more about magic. After all, it is a subject that is all about secrets! It is said that the door to magic is closed but not locked. Here are some ways of turning the handle.

LIBRARY

Look in your local library for information about magic – you will find books about its history and on new tricks you can learn.

MAGIC SHOPS

Many towns have magic shops. They will be advertized in your local phone directory under headings like MAGIC SHOPS or MAGIC DEALERS.

MAGAZINES

Magazines that specialize in magic can be very useful. Write for details on the following magazines to the addresses below:

Magic
Stan Allen & Associates,
7380 S. Eastern Avenue,
Suite 124–179, Las Vegas,
NV 89123, USA

Abracadabra
Goodliffe Publications,
150 New Road,
Bromsgrove,
Worcs. B60 2LG, UK

MAGIC CLUBS

Large towns and cities often have a magic club. They may be more difficult to find than the magic shops. If so, try phoning your nearest magic shop and asking them how to find a local magic club. Many clubs have sections for younger members.

The most famous magical society in the world is The Magic Circle in London. This has a postal club for young magicians all over the world. Write to:
The Young Magicians' Club,
The Magic Circle,
12 Stephenson Way,
London NW1 2HD, UK

THE INTERNET

On the Internet, there are probably more pages of information concerning magic and magicians than any other subject! Magicians are often as fascinated by computers as they are by magic!

FROM THE HORSE'S MOUTH

A good way to find out more about magic is to ask a visiting magician. But remember not to ask questions during the middle of a show!

INDEX

ACKNOWLEDGEMENTS

Kingfisher would like to thank the following people for their invaluable help: the staff at the magic shop Davenports for lending us equipment; Rachel Fuller for making the props; Marion McLornan for the special effects used in *Putting on a show*; Ray Moller and Sam Martin for their patience and expertise in the photographic studio; Jo Brown, Lisa Macdonald and Katie Puckett for buying essential equipment. Finally, we would like to say a very big thank you to all of the children who were our models: Aju Ahilan, Gurtaj and Janatpreet Bahd, Paul Bedford, Jay Briant, Tom Buddle, Antoine Campbell, Ben Clewley, Eleanor Davis, Cherelle Dovey (from Tiny Tots to Teens), Kaisha Esty, Thomas Gage, Connie Kirby (from Scallywags agency), Kiki Loizou, Henry and James Moller, Ross Parsons, Claire and Nicholas Tolman.